Why I Love Jesus

Why I Love Jesus

a personal testimony by

Frank Allred

Grace Publications

GRACE PUBLICATIONS TRUST
7 Arlington Way
London EC1R 1XA
England
e-mail: AGBCSE@aol.com

Managing Editors:
T. I. Curnow
M. J. Adams

First published 2007

ISBN 10: 0-94646-273-9
ISBN 13: 978-0-946462-73-5

Distributed by

EVANGELICAL PRESS
Faverdale North Industrial Estate
Darlington DL3 OPH
England
e-mail: sales@evangelicalpress.org
www.evangelicalpress.org

Printed and bound in Great Britain by
Biddles Ltd, King's Lynn, Norfolk

Contents

To the Reader

ON RETIRING NINETEEN YEARS AGO the last thing I wanted to do was to spend my time doing nothing in particular. My desire to serve the Lord was as strong as ever. But in what way? Since I had to retire because of heart trouble, what further use was my considerable experience in preaching and teaching the gospel? Falteringly, I made my request known to God – as if he didn't know already – asking him that I might still reach many people with the gospel during my retirement – perhaps even more than I did during my full time ministry. Was it too much to ask? It certainly seemed like it to me.

I know very well that God does not need me. He depends on no one. But in view of the way he had deigned to use me in the past, it seemed such a waste of time to spend my retirement seeking pleasure. Since I always had a desire to write, but never had the time to pursue it, I decided that now was the time to start.

Writing books is very different from preaching and teaching. The feedback is long delayed. The immediate response from the congregation is no longer there! It is a bit like putting messages in a bottle and dropping them in the ocean. Even so, I am deeply humbled when I receive letters from people in various parts of the world expressing their appreciation of my books. Obviously, my lack of faith limited my expectation.

Encouragement comes trickling through from unexpected quarters – a letter from a consultant in the south of England to say how he had been challenged by one of my books, letters in broken English from pastors in Africa asking for more, requests for permission to translate into other languages. Payment in gold bars would not be greater reward.

Since I am now 84, I decided it would not be wise to start writing longer books just in case I am not able to finish them. I shared this with a Christian friend who graciously rebuked me. 'No, no,' he said, 'you must not think like that.' His words were more powerful than he realised. Once again, my tendency to allow my age to restrict my vision was nipped in the bud.

This book is shorter, but not for that reason. My reasons for loving Jesus would fill a much larger volume, but here I want to focus on the basics. Having said that, however, it would not surprise me if the contents come as a surprise to some. My yearning to tell the world why I love Jesus has been bottled up for a long time, since I no longer have a pulpit. And opportunities to testify in today's secular society are rare. (How distressing it is that majority of people in this England, once proud to call itself Christian, lapse into silence when the name of Jesus is mentioned.)

My second motive for writing this book is to persuade Christian readers who may think of themselves as too old to be in the Master's service, to think again. The following verses from Psalm 92 have been a constant challenge and encouragement to me in my retirement: 'The righteous will flourish like a palm tree, they will grow like a cedar of Lebanon; planted in the house of the LORD, they will flourish in the courts of our God. *They will still bear fruit in old age, they will stay fresh and green*, proclaiming, "The LORD is upright; he is my Rock, and there is no wickedness in him"' (Ps. 92:12-15, emphasis added). As Derek Kidner puts it in his commentary on the Psalms (Psalms volume 2, Tyndale Commentaries, IVP, 1975), 'It is not the greenness of perpetual youth, but the freshness of age without sterility.'

You must not assume that I have been able to leap around like a ten-year old since I retired. So many parts of the old body are failing that I sometimes wonder how I manage to stay alive! Thankfully, my grey matter, such as it is, still works reasonably well.

Although I am filled with gratitude to God for the wonderful way in which he has guided me through life and used my limited talents for his glory, the book is not the story of my life. It focuses rather on what Jesus has done and is still doing for me. Inevitably, the pronoun 'I' appears frequently, but the reader must not assume that I take any credit for my privileged position. With Paul, I freely acknowledge that nothing good lives in me, that is, in my sinful nature (Rom. 7:18). All the changes for the better in my life are entirely due to the grace of God.

Christians these days tend to speak (and sing) more about their love for Jesus than his love for them. Given the title of the book, you may be surprised to know that I find myself at variance with the trend. For this reason I have been careful to emphasise that my love for Jesus is a response to his amazing love for me – a response that I could not give without his help and support. I love him because he first loved me. I love him because my name was linked with his before the world was made. I love him because he accomplished my redemption. I love him because he found me when I was lost and drew me to himself. I love him because he has promised never to leave me nor forsake me. I love him because he has gone to prepare a place for me, and is coming back to take me to be with him.

The reader must not think that I do not honour the Father as well. To bring glory to the Father it is necessary to honour the Son (John 5:23; Phil. 2:11). Jesus himself taught us that he who does not honour the Son does not honour the Father who sent him. No one can come to the Father except through the Lord Jesus.

I honour the Holy Spirit too. He is the one Person who prefers to stay out of the limelight but delights to reveal the Person of Christ. Without the Spirit's work in me, Jesus would have remained a stranger.

The book has its limitations, if only for the reason that the joy of loving Jesus and being loved by him cannot be expressed in words. The reader who has no experience of his love is like the man standing on the pavement in the brilliant sunshine, gazing at a stained glass window in the Cathedral. His friend was doing his best to describe its splendour, but to no avail. When they went inside the building and saw the beauty of the window as the sun shone through it from the outside, words were no longer necessary.

If I had my life over again I would spend it serving the Lord I love. Perhaps I would be a more faithful servant the second time round. But indulging in fantasy serves no useful purpose. Yet, as Paul said, 'I care very little if I am judged by you or by any human court; indeed, I do not judge myself. My conscience is clear, but that does not make me innocent. It is the Lord who judges me' (1 Cor. 4:3-4). I know that the love of Jesus is unconditional and I know that his death covers all my sins. Therefore, 'for to me, to live is Christ and to die is gain' (Phil. 1:21).

To avoid awkward phrases, I regard the reader as male, but no discrimination is intended.

1.
I Love Jesus Because
He Loves Me

I SHALL NEVER FORGET the day my mother caught me with my hand in the till. My family lived behind a shop, and the only way into the street was through the shop. Every time the shop door opened, a bell rang in the house. I thought I was able to open the till quickly and quietly as I passed behind the counter, without arousing suspicion. After I got away with it several times, my confidence increased and it became a habit. But my mother must have noticed that the time it took for me to go through the shop was a little longer than it should have been.

Across the clear glass window of the door separating the shop from the living quarters, a curtain was drawn. By drawing back this curtain slightly, it was possible to see if anyone was in the shop. One day, out of the corner of my eye, with my hand still in the till, I saw the curtains move. I turned and looked straight into my mother's eyes. It is now seventy years ago, but the image of her disapproving face behind the window is indelibly etched in my memory.

After the severe reprimand, the matter was never mentioned again. It was as if it had not happened, although I do not doubt that my behaviour caused my parents much grief. Stealing was certainly not my only vice. Yet, in spite of it all, I still felt loved and secure. The thought that my parents might stop loving me because of my waywardness never crossed my mind. It was not until later years that I realised how vital for my development their constancy was in this matter. They just never stopped loving me.

The love of Jesus is like this, except that his love is perfect. If my sins grieved my parents, how much more do they offend my Saviour, who is untainted by sin? Yet, he loves me with an unwavering and unfailing holy love. He has promised never to leave me

or forsake me (Heb. 13:5). Now that I am the adopted child of his
Father and mine (Gal. 4:5), Jesus is my brother (Heb. 2:11).

Moreover, the love of Jesus is timeless, whereas my parents' love
for me endured for about fifty years. Although the memory of it is
vivid, it is still but a memory. By contrast, Jesus loved me before I
was born. Indeed, he loved me before the world was born – before
time began (Eph. 1:4). Back in eternity, my name was engraved on
his heart because I am one of those people who were given by the
Father to his Son (John 17:24). Privileged am I beyond measure,
because it was God's plan to unite me with his Son in an unbreak-
able relationship. It is from this marvellous source that all my blessings spring.

I glory in the Christ of the cross because it was for me he suffered and died. For without question, all the blessings planned for
me were conferred on me by his death. It was for me that he endured the agony of separation from his Father! It was to seal the
covenant with his blood. What amazing condescension! What inexpressible love!

I freely acknowledge that it was the Holy Spirit who opened
my mind to appreciate this. It was he who portrayed Christ crucified before my eyes (Gal. 3:1). In comparison, my love for him is
weak. Even so, my soul clings to him, my mind delights in him, and
my heart's desire is to be like him. From the knowledge of his sacrifice for me comes, not only the awareness of the depravity in my
sinful nature, but also my assurance of ultimate victory over it.

What did I do to deserve my parents' love? Nothing! They
loved me because I was their child. What did I do to become their
child? Nothing! Again, the same is true of the love of Jesus. Since
the privilege of being loved by him was conferred on me *before* I was
born, how could I possibly do anything to merit it? Why then, you
may ask, should I be so privileged? Why indeed?! Only God knows
the answer to that. That a rebel like me should share the glory of
God with his beloved Son is beyond human understanding.

You will see therefore, that I have absolutely nothing to boast
about. I am deeply grateful that it was according to the Father's
will that I should receive full and free forgiveness of all my sins,
together with the gift of the Holy Spirit and the sure and certain

hope of being like Jesus in his glorious presence. Further than that, I cannot go.

The fact that I am a beneficiary of the divine will is, however, a most powerful incentive for me to love him. The more I have been able to get my mind round the wonder of God's sovereign grace demonstrated in the death of Christ, the stronger this incentive has become. With that delightful development, however, comes a feeling of regret because I could have been more zealous in God's service. How much more devoted to it I would have been if my understanding and appreciation of his love had been what it is today. I have been an unprofitable servant, and I cannot go back and make good the loss.

You should not think for a moment that my love for Jesus is a *natural* response to all these benefits. On the contrary, I have no natural affection for him whatever. Left to my own devices, I would either hate him or ignore him, as do the rest of unbelievers in the world (Rom. 7:21-25). Indeed, such is my sinful nature, that I still find myself doing those things that displease him. This evil part of me would willingly join the crowds who shouted 'crucify him' at the top of their voices.

But that is no longer possible because he has poured out his love into my heart by the Holy Spirit whom he has given to me (Rom. 5:5). Therefore, the strong desire in my heart to love and serve the Lord Jesus is not my own doing. So weak and vulnerable am I, that apart from his love I would not be able to love him. And apart from his constant care (1 Peter 5:7), it would be impossible to make any progress towards my high calling. Falling away, however, is out of the question because his love will never let me go. In his love, I am perfectly safe (John 10:29), and that forever.

2.

I Love Jesus Because
He Drew Me to Himself

A FRIEND OF MINE ONCE ASKED ME a rather difficult question. 'What first attracts a man to a woman?' The inclusion of the word 'first' ruled out such things as her wisdom, her ability or her kind disposition. These qualities take longer to assess. I concluded that the answer must have something to do with her pretty face, or perhaps her attractive figure. My friend, who was a married woman, insisted it was a pretty face. Her husband agreed.

Now if you ask me what first attracted me to Jesus, I would find myself in a different world altogether. My answer would have nothing to do with his physical appearance because I don't know what he looked like. The Bible suggests that, as a man, there was nothing particularly impressive or attractive about him (Isa. 53:2). Nor would it have anything to do with his perfect character because even though I had learned a lot about the good things he did and the wonders he performed, I was not the slightest bit interested.

Left to my own devices, it would have been easier to draw blood from a stone than for me to respond to the love of Jesus. Oh yes, I had that much vaunted power to choose, but like the rest of mankind I never chose what I did not want to choose. Obviously, if I were forced to make choices that were contrary to my wishes and to my reason, they would not be free choices. For the same reason, if I made a decision to follow Christ against my will, it would not be a free choice. Therefore, we must look for the answer to the question elsewhere.

Before we do, let us go back for a moment to the question of love between the sexes. The other day another friend, now in his seventies and still single, was telling me about the time he fell head over heels in love. Being a modest person, he did not tell the woman concerned how much he admired her and craved her company. One day, when he was enjoying one of the few conversations he had with her, she referred, quite casually, to her husband. It was a bombshell! A protracted struggle with his emotions followed, but my friend eventually came to terms with the situation. He has never felt the same about any other woman, perhaps because he thinks there could be no one else like the one he loved.

Now here is a man who had to make a decision that was contrary to his deepest longing. Or was it? It was certainly contrary to his burning desire to pursue a relationship with the woman he loved, but since he was a Christian, it was not contrary to his desire to please God. This gives rise to an interesting question. Where did the two conflicting desires come from? Clearly, his desire to be with the woman was a natural response to what he saw in her. It arose within himself. But his love for Jesus and his desire to please God was not natural. It was God the Holy Spirit who put it there.

The answer then to the question as to what first attracted me to Jesus is to be found in Jesus and not in me. It was he, by his Spirit, who opened my eyes to see his beauty. He made me understand how much he loved me, and what he did to save me (Gal. 2:20). My natural desires were elsewhere. As the old hymn says, he drew me with the cords of love, and thus he bound me to him. There is no other explanation.

Without doubt, the dramatic change was a miracle. Within a very short time, my habit of using the name of Jesus in blasphemy was displaced by a desire to honour his name and to follow him. From being his enemy, I became his friend. The power of my former antagonism was completely broken so that I was able, gladly and freely, to choose to love him. Now, sixty-six years on, those cords of love are stronger than ever. Nothing in the world compares with the joy of knowing Jesus. Yet, none of it would ever have happened without the gracious wooing of the Holy Spirit.

The bitter disappointment of unrequited love such as my friend suffered can never be the experience of those who are drawn to Jesus. Since it is his Father who draws us, Jesus will receive us (John 6:44). And since God gave us to his Son by an eternal and unchangeable decree (John 17:6,20), who or what can come between us? (Rom. 8:39) This means that my love relationship with Jesus can never end.

I hope you do not rebel against the idea of God drawing me to himself, especially when it is clear that he does not do this for others. Many people get rather hot under the collar about the idea of God doing the choosing, especially when others are passed over. They regard it as flagrant violation of their will.

If you are tempted to think this way – or to entertain ideas that God is not being fair – you need to know that you have no right to accuse God of injustice. 'Shall what is formed say to him who formed it, "Why did you make me like this?" Does not the potter have the right to make out of the same lump of clay some pottery for noble purposes and some for common use?' (Rom. 9:20,21). God owes us nothing.

You will be the person who will be hurt most by reacting in this way. If, on the other hand, you are persuaded that God the Father takes the initiative in the matter of our salvation, it may well be a sign that God is already at work in your life. A genuine desire to know God never originates in the human heart.

When I first came to Jesus, he accepted me just as he promised. The question as to whether or not I was chosen never occurred to me. Yet, it was not long before I willingly acknowledged that he loved me long before I gave him a thought (1 John 4:19). Is it not evident then, that he drew me because he chose me? Is it not obvious that spiritual blessings were lavished on me because God predetermined that it should be so?

3.

I Love Jesus Because
He Opened My Mind to Understand the Scriptures

If $ax^2+bx+c=0$, $x=\dfrac{-b\pm\sqrt{(b^2 - 4ac)}}{2a}$

I AM HOPELESS AT MATHEMATICS, so please don't ask me what this means. My wife knows what it is all about, but she was a maths teacher. Now imagine what it would be like if I were provided with a pair of magic spectacles so that, without any training, I was suddenly able to understand it. Joseph Smith, founder of the Mormon movement, was supposedly given just such spectacles and was then able to read the ancient script in which the Book of Mormon was written. It is the stuff of fairy tales.

Yet, the Holy Spirit performed a miracle in me that enabled me to read and understand the Scriptures. He did it, not by providing magic spectacles, but by opening my mind to the truth. Many times before my conversion I had tried to understand the Bible, but without success. To read it was a bit like trying to eat tasteless food when one is not hungry.

The very day after my conversion, however, everything changed. The word came to life, and its meaning began to thrill my heart. The passages I had known by heart for many years but did not understand suddenly came alive with meaning. I discovered that in so many places it was talking about me and to me. It was explaining in graphic detail what had happened in my life. And as God's word became real to me, so God himself became real to me. Everywhere I looked in the Book, I was able to discern his beauty and excellence.

In the first verse of John's Gospel, we are introduced to the mystery of the Holy Trinity. John tells us that Jesus is the Word, and that he *was* (in existence) at the beginning of creation. This means that Jesus had no beginning. The apostle goes on to say that the Word was with God, and that the Word was God (John 1:1). Get your mind round that if you can! But it is not difficult to understand why Jesus is called 'the Word.' God the Father planned to reveal himself through his Son. Therefore, to see Jesus is to see the Father, as Jesus said (John 14:9). God has spoken to us by his Son (Heb. 1:1).

Therefore, from my conversion right through to the present time, the living Word and the written word have been inseparable. How can it be otherwise when Jesus, the living Word is revealed through the written word, and nowhere else?

I also discovered why I could not understand the Scriptures before. The person who does not have the Spirit does not accept what the Spirit teaches. They are foolishness to him because being without the Spirit he *cannot* understand them (1 Cor. 2:14). The apostle is insisting that to the unconverted man, the Scriptures are dull and distasteful. Notice too, that Paul is saying that the unspiritual man cannot understand them, not merely that he does not or will not. That is how it was with me in those far off days when I did not know the Lord.

I praise God, just as Jesus did, because the Lord of heaven and earth has hidden these things from the wise and learned, and revealed them to little children (Matt. 11:25). If a high intelligence quotient had been necessary, I would have remained ignorant. But when Jesus referred to the 'wise and the learned' he was talking about those who are worldly wise and over confident about their intellectual ability. The 'little children' may be unlearned and simple people, but unlike all others, they understand the Spirit's teaching.

Because of my firm trust in the Scriptures, a bishop of the Church of England once accused me of having a closed mind. 'What you need Allred', he said, 'is a more open mind.' It was obvious to me that the boot was on the other foot. The bishop's mind was closed completely to the truth of God's written word. Clergymen like me, who believed God's word, were an embarrassment to him, and he seldom missed an opportunity to snipe at me. Poor man!

4.

I Love Jesus Because
He Showed Me What I Was Really Like

NOT FAR FROM WHERE I LIVE there is an old Victorian building known as the Clock Tower Café. About two years ago, vandals climbed up the steep roof, breaking the tiles as they went. They twisted the hands of the clock and put it out of action. When I saw what they had done, I was filled with indignation. 'These stupid teenagers', I said to myself, 'what is the world coming to?' Abruptly, my grumbling stopped. I remembered what I did to other people's property when I was a young teenager. I have vivid memories of removing the light bulbs in the train as I travelled to and from school, and throwing them against the tunnel wall as the train passed through. How easy it is to pass judgment on others when we are guilty of the same things.

I also remember breaking into the pavilion belonging to the church cricket club, not once but several times, and drinking the ginger ale from the large stone bottles that were kept there for the benefit of thirsty cricketers. Of course, I was always accompanied by other teenagers who were just as delinquent as I was.

If you have a desire to hear more of my escapades, I would have no difficulty in satisfying your wish, but it would not be appropriate. I do not want to give the impression that I am proud of what I did. On the contrary, I am thoroughly ashamed.

Ah! You say, with that kind of behaviour you needed to be converted. This is true, but you would be wrong to assume that I was in greater need than anyone else. Our sinful nature finds expression in very different ways, but the fact remains that we have all sinned and fallen short of God's standard (Rom. 3:23). Our sinfulness does not merely relate to our sinful acts, but to our sinful hearts. If the condition itself were cured, the symptoms would look after themselves.

It was necessary therefore that the Holy Spirit should not merely remind me of my misdemeanours. He had to convince me that there was nothing good – good in the sight of God – in me. He graciously and lovingly brought me to agree with the verdict of Scripture that there is nothing more deceitful than the human heart and that the condition is incurable (Jer. 17:9). It was not a pleasant experience.

Ever since that day however, I have had no difficulty in identifying with the apostle Paul when he describes himself as 'a wretched man'. 'Who will rescue me from this body of death?' he cries (Rom. 7:24). Nor would I ever want to disagree with the verdict of Jesus that evil thoughts, murder, adultery, sexual immorality, theft, false testimony, slander come from the heart (Matt. 15:19). He was not speaking just about muggers and murderers but about you and me.

Also since that day, I have had the opportunity to observe the violent reaction of people, – especially religious people – when confronted with the verdict of Scripture. Indeed, the minister of the gospel who tells his congregation that all have sinned, and that their 'good' deeds contribute nothing towards their salvation, must prepare himself for an angry response. It is not easy for self-righteous religious people to accept that heaven is a gift and not a reward for their 'good' deeds (Eph. 2:9).

One man I remember was so enraged, he came storming into the church vestry at the end of a service with his sleeves pulled back and both his fists clenched. He demanded to know what right I had to call him a sinner! In the service, I had simply explained that we have no merit in the sight of God and that even our righteous acts are like filthy rags in God's sight (Isa. 64:6). The fact that he had taken it personally was not my doing!

The reason for this kind of reaction is that the seriousness of our natural condition is never realised unless the Spirit of God begins to work as he did in me. Unless he reveals the evil that controls our thoughts and actions, we shall forever remain wilfully ignorant of it. Yet, the condition is more deadly than any physical illness, more lethal than any virus, and more harmful than any handicap, physical or mental.

A friend of mine used to say that if a colour film of his thoughts during the course of a single day were shown on TV, he would never be able to look his friends in the face again. No doubt, his friends would have suffered the same humiliation if it happened to them. The fear of being thus exposed, together with the felt need to maintain a respectable image, motivates us to keep our wicked thoughts to ourselves.

What a strange anomaly it is then, that in spite of the fact that evil in some form is active in our hearts, we still have a foolish tendency to claim that we are good. We are accomplished in the art of convincing ourselves of this and refuse to consider that the truth might be otherwise. It is evidence of our sinful nature at work.

I was no exception, until the gravity of the corruption in my heart stared me in the face. Trying to make light of it was no longer an option. How thankful I am for this! Had it not happened I would never have seen the beauty and glory of my Saviour Jesus. I would never have been awakened to my desperate need of him.

I suppose in later life, I might have gained some respectability, but where would that have taken me? On the other hand, I may have become dissolute. I just do not know. Nor am I very interested. What I do know is that Jesus has delivered me from the consequences of being under the control of my sinful nature and so from the torments of hell. That is why I love him.

5.

I Love Jesus Because
He Gave Me the Ability to Repent

MANY YEARS AGO I PARKED MY CAR IN THE STREET outside the house where I lived. It was broad daylight. About two hours later when it was dark, I answered a knock at the door and found myself face to face with a burly police officer. At that time, the parking of cars without lights in the street at night was illegal and the law was enforced. Immediately I realised what the problem was and apologised profusely, but the officer was not inclined to give me a second chance.

As it happened, my work brought me into regular contact with the local Criminal Investigation Department, so I asked one of the detectives what I should do. He advised me to write to the Chief Constable and apologise unconditionally. In other words, I should not try to make excuses. I did as I was advised and by return of post, I received a letter from the Chief to say that I would be excused this time, but if there were any further infringements of the law, he would be obliged to take the present offence into account.

Do you think my apology was sincere? I was truly sorry, but only because I had been caught. In reality, my letter was a device to try to avoid prosecution. It certainly could not be called an act of repentance because it did not come from my heart. Truth to tell, I was a little irritated by the police officer's intransigence.

How different it was when God knocked on my door – in this case the door of my heart – and accused me of infringing his law! It was not an isolated case either. Indeed, the whole tenor of my life fell far short of his standard. For the first time in my life, I understood how grievous my sin was (and still is) in the sight of a holy God. I became aware, also for the first time, of a strong desire to renounce sin and to live a new life.

Ever since I was knee high to a duck, as they used to say in Lancashire, I needed no one to tell me that I was far from perfect. Many times, I tried to change myself without success. Do-It-Yourself reformations are never successful because the power of the human will is not up to it. I disapproved in particular of my foul mouth. Indeed, such was my determination to rid myself of this offensive habit that I adopted methods that were supposed to assist the will in defeating it. It was all to no avail. More times than I can count, I came face to face with my utter helplessness. Sin was my master.

Thank God, however, that when the Spirit showed me my sinful self, he did not leave me in this miserable condition. With the sense of guilt came an intense awareness that full and free forgiveness was being offered to me. I knew all about Jesus dying for the sins of the world, but now it became personal. It was for *my* sins that he died. He bore the punishment that was justly mine.

At that time, I knew nothing about the arguments for and against irresistible grace – the teaching that when God is at work in the heart of a sinner, he does not have the ability to resist. As far as I am concerned, the last thing I wanted was an option to refuse. I can only conclude that God's grace was indeed irresistible, and I am delighted that it was so. I freely embraced the offer with gratitude.

Further, although I did not fully understand the implications at the time, I knew that my desire to live a different life was really a longing to be like Jesus. Now, as I come near to the end of my life on earth, that longing is still with me. Indeed, of all the yearnings that have gripped me throughout my life, my desire to be like Jesus is now the strongest. What a joy it is to know that one day it will be fully satisfied (1 John 3:2).

As I began to know more of the Scriptures, I realised that repentance and faith are two sides of the same coin. They belonged together at the beginning of my Christian life and they still belong together at the end. Repentance may precede faith in our experience or vice versa, but they cannot work independently of each other.

Often, as I sit at my computer, I am amazed at the technology behind it. In so many fields man's ability is astonishing. Yet, even though he can produce microcircuits, he cannot repent and believe of his own volition. He can go to the moon but he cannot stop himself being proud, selfish or dishonest. He cannot even tame his tongue. As the apostle James said so long ago, we can steer large ships with a small rudder, but we cannot control the tongue (James 3:4,8). When the opportunity presents itself, the evil in the human heart will always find expression.

I love Jesus then, because when I was unable to understand the gravity of my sin and too weak to repent and believe, he came to my rescue. Unlike those escapologists who wriggle and squirm to get out of their straitjackets and chains, my fetters simply fell off. As Charles Wesley puts it in one of his well-known hymns: 'My chains fell off, my heart was free. I rose, went forth, and followed Thee.'

You must not think that God gave me the capacity to repent and believe just once, at my conversion. Once given, the gift has never been withdrawn so that for me, to go on believing is to go on repenting. The person who does not repent of his sins cannot be a true believer. Although my repentance has not always been as prompt as it should have been, whenever I turn to him and confess my sins, he readily forgives (1 John 1:9).

Repentance has always affected my emotions. Sorrow for sin never failed to bring feelings of remorse. Yet, the Godly sorrow has always been accompanied by (or followed by) inexpressible joy – joy that is the result of the assurance of forgiveness. My experience teaches me that without godly sorrow, it is not possible to have a strong assurance of eternal life. Nothing undermines the believer's hope like the failure to repent.

Why, you may ask, does my love for Jesus not stop me from sinning against him? There are two closely connected reasons: First, compared with his constant love for me, my love for him blows hot and cold. I grieve deeply about this and look forward to the day when Jesus will rescue me from this corrupt body (Rom. 7:24-25). Second, as much as I hate it, sinful thoughts and actions plague me daily, and will do so as long as I am in this body (Rom. 7:21).

What a calamity it would have been if God, after giving me the ability to repent at my conversion, left me to repent on my own thereafter! My latter condition would have been worse than the first. As it is, he will never allow me to be anything other than perturbed about my sins and he never fails to grant repentance and forgiveness. His mercy is endless.

Indeed, in my later years I have discovered that the more I know of the love of Jesus, the deeper my repentance becomes. Sorrow for sins of the past, even the distant past, has been far more acute in my old age. This does not mean that I have become more morose. On the contrary, my delight in the fellowship of my forgiving Saviour coexists with my godly sorrow. As well as being a distinct action when circumstances demand it, repentance is now an attitude of life. I know that nothing I do is perfect, even when I am not aware of it. Only those readers who experience these things will grasp what I am talking about.

The Lord does not think much of the self-righteous person who persists in fooling himself about his true condition. By contrast, he thinks highly of the man whose spirit is wounded because of his sin and whose repentance goes deep into his soul. God is pleased with him because, in spite of his weakness, he has a humble and contrite spirit, and trembles at God's word (Isa. 66:2b). How gracious is our God!

6.

I Love Jesus Because
He Removed My Guilt

SIGMUND FREUD (1856-1939) BELIEVED THAT, far from being a gift from God, conscience was the conditioning of the mind by external influences. Our sense of right and wrong was developed from the standards set by our parents and the society in which we were brought up. He also believed that the 'conscience' frequently acted in a repressive manner, creating destructive feelings of guilt.

This will not do. We would all agree that conscience is not an infallible judge of our actions and motives. Indeed, it is possible to stifle the voice of conscience to such an extent that it becomes silent. This is what Paul meant when he spoke about people whose consciences have been seared as with a hot iron (1 Tim. 4:2). But conscience is much more than a faculty formed by external influences. It is God's gift.

Our dog's 'conscience' was a conditioned reflex. He knew he was forbidden to do certain things, like putting his head on the knees of guests sitting at the table and looking pitifully into their eyes in the hope of being fed a crumb or two. He never had a conscience about it, because morality did not come into it. He would try anything if he thought he could get away with it. His tail only went between his legs when he was rebuked. We, however, are not like animals. Our consciences pronounce *moral* judgments on our actions, something that never happens in animals.

I think of the conscience as a room. The sunlight is shining through the window and showing up all the dark and dusty corners. The process of stifling the conscience begins when no action is taken to deal with what the light reveals – ignoring those dusty corners for example. If the neglect continues, the curtains begin to close until eventually the dust is no longer visible. The end result is total darkness.

I am thankful because in spite of my waywardness in early life, the curtains did not close in my inner room. On the contrary, my conscience remained reasonably tender. By 'tender', I do not mean weak. A weak conscience will produce guilty feelings when there is nothing to feel guilty about. This was not the case with me. I had a lot to feel guilty about. Perhaps the time was coming when my conscience would have become less efficient, but God had mercy on me before that happened.

In later life, I still find myself praying that the Lord will keep my conscience tender, even if at times I have violated it under pressure of temptation. Of course, as a believer, God has given me a hunger for his word so that I have been a serious student of the Bible for very many years. Being familiar with its contents guarantees that my conscience remains efficient (Heb. 5:14).

Feeling guilty and being guilty are very different. God's standards being far higher than ours, we are guilty of many things we never *feel* guilty about. In our ignorance, we are not always aware of our sins. God's commandments determine our guilt, not the conscience. To think that we are no longer guilty if the sins that cause us to *feel* guilty are forgiven is folly in the extreme.

Guilt does not only arise from what I do, but also from what I think. I am guilty before God because of past thoughts as well as actions that fell short of his standard. I am also guilty because of my failure to act when it was my duty to do so. Nothing I can do will change my guilty status. Every human being is guilty whether he feels it or not, because all have failed to keep God's commandments. I need no persuading that apart from God's mercy my case is hopeless. By nature I am a transgressor and liable to punishment.

Now, I love Jesus because he has removed all my guilt. He has cleansed all my sins; not only those I have a conscience about, but also those I do not even know about. Surprising as it may seem, he has forgiven my future sins as well. This means that all my guilt – my past guilt, present guilt, and future guilt – has been taken away.

Now if you should think that this means I can sin as much as I like, you would merely be advertising the fact that you are a stranger to divine mercy. The fact is I now have a strong desire to please God, a desire given to me by the Holy Spirit. Like every other believer, I am still plagued by my sinful nature, but God has given me a new nature so that I delight in his commandments (Rom. 7:25). Why should I deliberately grieve the One who loves me so much? And since I now love him for what he has done for me, how can I enjoy sinning against him? If I do sin, he gives me no peace until I repent. This is not pleasant, but I am continually grateful for it.

You may also think that to let a guilty sinner go free is contrary to divine justice. You would be right. It is also contrary to natural justice. How often we hear vociferous complaints from the public when judges allow offenders to go free, or pass a light sentence for a serious crime!

The truth is, however, that God did not violate his justice when he removed my guilt. Since Christ, who knew no sin, paid the penalty for me, all my guilt has been put to his account. I am no longer guilty in God's eyes (Gal. 3:13). The demands of divine justice have all been fully satisfied.

Being justified before God is of course much more than being forgiven. It means that my legal status before him has changed. Christ's perfect righteousness is now reckoned as mine. 'Blessed is the man whose sin the Lord will never count against him' (Rom. 4:8).

7.

I Love Jesus Because
He Rescued Me from the Fire

I VIVIDLY RECALL A FIRE AT A RETAIL STORE in Manchester. Members of the staff were trapped on the top floor of the building. They tried to use the lift, but the fire had already engulfed the shaft. The staircase too was well alight. Their last option was the windows, but they were fitted with steel bars to prevent burglary. After a brave effort by the fire-fighters, some were brought down the ladder to safety but others perished in the flames before they could be reached. What a relief it must have been for those who were saved when they realised they were coming down the ladder on a fireman's shoulder to safety. How would they find words to express their gratitude?

This is how I feel about Jesus. He saved me from something much more terrible than physical death in a fire. He delivered me from the torments of hell where the fire never goes out (Mark 9:43). Oh yes, hell is a real place because Jesus himself said so. Whether he was speaking figuratively or not when he warned us about the unquenchable fire is of little consequence. Either way, he was telling us that hell is a terrible place. To make fun of the idea, as many do, is to make fun of Jesus, and that is a very foolish thing to do.

In New Testament times, a valley near Jerusalem called Gehenna was used as a rubbish tip. Children had been burned alive there in sacrifice to heathen gods. It was also a place where the corpses of criminals were burned. The fire never went out. Because it was such a ghastly place, Gehenna became the Greek word for 'hell', and this is the word used in many translations of the New Testament. Some use expressions like 'the fire of hell' or 'the Gehenna of fire'.

My wife and I used to go to the Criccieth area of North Wales for holidays. At that time, between Criccieth and Portmadoc, a rubbish tip was always burning, and the rising column of smoke could be seen for miles around. Every time I saw it, the horrors of Gehenna came to mind, along with a solemn verse in the Book of Revelation that speaks about those who die without Christ. It tells us that the smoke of their torment rises for ever and ever (Rev. 14:11).

Scripture also speaks of hell as a place of darkness. This too may be symbolic, but again it reminds us that hell is a place of despair and hopelessness – a place to which all who do not repent and believe the gospel will be banished. It is a place of darkness because the light of God's presence never penetrates the place. Without light, there is no life and no joy.

Whenever we speak of being saved from anything – like drowning, burning, bankruptcy and so forth – we always use the passive voice. This is because whatever it is we are saved from, it is always due to the intervention of others. If we find ourselves in deep water and cannot swim, we need someone to pull us out. If we are on the point of being declared bankrupt, we need someone to give us some cash. We cannot save ourselves.

This is why Christians use the passive voice when they speak of their salvation. Jesus left his Father's glory, which he had enjoyed from eternity past, and was born into this world of sin for a single purpose – to save sinners. 'Here is a trustworthy saying' says Paul, '... Christ Jesus came into the world to save sinners' (1 Tim. 1:15). He did the saving, and we are the ones he saved.

Then the apostle adds these surprising words: 'of whom I am the worst'. No doubt, there were many people worse than Paul, but this is not the point. The apostle had progressed in the Christian life to the stage where he never ceased to be amazed at the magnitude of God's grace. Inevitably, this had the effect of making him much more conscious of his sinful condition.

That is how I feel about myself, and for the same reason. The more I learn about God's infinite grace in saving me from the fire, the more I feel the gravity of my sin. Seen in this light, any claim to a righteousness of my own is utterly absurd. All the credit and all the praise for my deliverance must go to where it belongs – to the Lord Jesus alone.

8.

I Love Jesus Because He Conquered Death for Me

DEATH, LIKE HELL, IS NOT PLEASANT. It generates grief and pain and brings everything to an untimely end. It is always threatening. It is the point at which our eternal destiny is fixed, one way or the other, for there can be no further opportunity to repent and believe. The Roman Catholic teaching about the place called Purgatory, where sinners endure temporary punishment before being admitted to heaven, is pure make-believe. It has no Biblical warrant.

Unbelievers may regard death as a necessity because if people did not die there would be no room in the world for future generations. But death is much more than a provider of space. The Bible tells us that death came into the world because of sin. If there were no sin, there would be no death. It is therefore a menace, an adversary, and a destroyer.

Death may strike at any time and at any age. A dear friend of mine dedicated his life to serve as a missionary doctor. After six years training and a further year studying theology, he got married and went out to Africa. After a few weeks, he was killed in a road accident. His car left the road and hit a tree.

Some years ago, I went to see my doctor about my inability to sleep. He gave me a thorough examination and some medication, and told me to come back in a week. As I was leaving, he said: 'Now you know what Job had to put up with.' These were the last words he spoke to me. A few days later, he had a heart attack and died. He was forty-one.

What a waste, we say. Why does God allow such things to happen? But is death not a waste whenever it occurs? We speak of death from 'natural causes' to distinguish it from death by accident or murder. But is death ever natural? To spend many years acquiring knowledge and experience so that we become experts in our field, and then die at the peak of our usefulness is most unnatural.

What is natural about the painful severing of a loving relationship just when it has reached maturity? What is natural about having hopes and plans for the future that are never realised because our lives are cut short? What is natural about being born to live under the shadow of death, not knowing when or where it will strike? Small wonder then, that the Bible describes death as 'the last enemy' (1 Cor. 15:26).

I mention all this because there was a time when the thought of death struck terror into my heart. In spite of my waywardness, I knew that my sins gave death the power to hurt me (1 Cor. 15:56) and that one day God would bring me to judgment. Nor did I need any reminding that death would deprive me of further opportunities to repent and believe.

This was the root cause of my fear. 'How did you handle it?', you may ask. By doing what most people do. I convinced myself that death was so far away, I had no need to worry, at least not yet. Tomorrow would be soon enough. So, wretch that I was, I persisted in my sinful ways. My friends were no different, so why should I be different and stick out like a sore thumb?

Jesus changed all that. He banished the fear of death for me. I no longer see it as a door into outer darkness and uncertainty, but a gateway into the presence of Jesus. Sin gives death its sting, but now that my sins are forgiven, the sting has been drawn (1 Cor. 15:56). The Lord Jesus removed it by bearing my punishment. Once my guilt was removed, the terrors of death were vanquished, and in place of that harassing fear, God has given me a sure and certain hope that as soon as I leave this body, I shall be with Christ, which is far better (Phil. 1:23).

There is more. The day is coming when Christ will come again and all the dead will be raised. Those who have done good will rise to live, and those who have done evil will rise to be condemned (John 5:28-29). But wait – does this mean that eternal life is a reward for my good deeds? Certainly not. It lays down the principle that all who are saved by grace show it by their holy lives. Those who claim to be true Christians but continue to do evil will rise to be condemned like the rest of the unbelieving world.

At the risk of being monotonous, I must emphasis yet again that I do not deserve to live forever. I am qualified to do so only because I am clothed in the righteousness of Christ. God caused his sinless Son to be regarded as a sinner, so that in him, I might be regarded as righteous. My sins are laid on him who bore them willingly, and his perfect righteousness is credited to me (2 Cor. 5:21).

So just as Jesus rose again from the dead, I too will rise (1 Thess. 4:16). Since death no longer has power over him, it no longer has power over me. Of course, my body must die. Until death is conquered, physical death will remain the consequence of human sin. It is a defeated foe, however, and when Jesus comes it will be banished forever.

I cannot claim to be completely free of fear about the *manner* of my death. Having suffered myself and ministered to many dying people who were in acute distress, some apprehension remains. I am not proud of this, but I must be honest.

Nevertheless, I have confidence that no matter how and when death occurs, it cannot separate me from his love (Rom. 8:38-39). The Lord Jesus has robbed death of its terrors, and I know that when this perishable body is clothed with the imperishable, death will be swallowed up in victory (1 Cor. 15:54).

9.
I Love Jesus Because
He Opened the Way to the Father

WHEN I CONTEMPLATE THE SHEER BEAUTY of God's creation and the amazing precision of its working, I sometimes feel it must be a dream. How could something so wonderful be real? Inevitably, at such times, the teaching of Paul comes quickly to my mind. God is angry, says the apostle, with those who wickedly suppress the truth about him – truths that are revealed in his creation. What may be known about God, Paul continues, is plain to them because God has made it plain to them. God's eternal power and divine nature are clearly seen, so that men are without excuse if they do not give thanks to him (Rom. 1:18-21). My emotional reaction to Paul's words is always a mixture of sorrow and anger towards those clever but blinded men who try to convince us that it all started with a big bang.

The day dawned when I witnessed another miracle. This time it was actually taking place in my own life. Again, I observed God's handiwork, but this time I saw much more of him than I had ever seen in creation. I discovered that there is all the difference in the world between knowing about God and knowing God. I realised that knowing about God is nothing more than data in the mind, but knowing him is a life-changing experience. How then, you may ask, did it happen?

On the first day of creation when thick darkness enveloped the earth, God said: 'Let there be light' and there was light. Total darkness is something we seldom experience because even on the darkest night there is always a glimmer of light. I think my last experience of it was in a hotel. We were on holiday and the film in my camera had jammed. I went into the hotel toilet, which happily had no windows, and switched off the light. The darkness was so intense, I felt bewildered and my eyes began to play tricks on me. This is what it must have been like before God uttered those four words: 'let there be light.'

When, by the grace of God, I was drawn to the Lord Jesus, the sequence of events was similar to the events leading up to creation. Just as God said, 'let there be light' and his light penetrated the thick darkness that covered the earth, so by his command the darkness that enveloped my mind and heart was dispersed. This was not merely a better intellectual understanding – far from it. The light of the knowledge of God illuminated my life and I saw him in a completely new way. It was the beginning of a real and personal relationship with God that I did not think possible – a relationship that has deepened over the years.

Paul puts it beautifully: 'For God, who said, "Let light shine out of darkness," made his light shine in our hearts to give us the light of the knowledge of the glory of God in the face of Christ' (2 Cor. 4:6).

Seeing God's eternal power and divine nature in his creation, wonderful as it is, was not enough. It still speaks to me about God, but it never tells me that he is a Person whom I may know as my Father. It leaves me without excuse if I fail to honour him, but if that were the end of the matter, God would remain unknown and unknowable. It is a sad fact that millions see God in his creation and therefore believe in his existence, but they do not know him as a Person. Before the light of Christ shined upon me, that was my position.

Now, I rejoice daily because Jesus has done for me what I could never do for myself. In Jesus, God is revealed to me as a Person who knows me through and through and who may be known. By removing the enmity between God and me, Jesus has granted me access to God the Father. This means I have freedom to approach him in the Name of Jesus at any time (Eph. 2:18). It also means that God now looks on me with favour.

Only Jesus could do this for me. He is the one who said, 'I am the way and the truth and the life. *No one comes to the Father except through me.*' There is no other way, no matter what counter claims are made. 'If you really knew me,' Jesus said, 'you would know my Father as well' (John 14:6-7).

In Old Testament times, a huge curtain was drawn between the inner and outer rooms of the temple. The room behind the curtain was most holy. Although the priests entered regularly into the outer room to carry on their ministry, only the high priest entered the inner room, and then only once a year (Heb. 9:6-12). It symbolised the very presence of God. The high priest always took with him the blood of the sacrifice that he had offered for his own sins and the sins of the people.

God intended this as an illustration of the better things to come. Jesus ascended into heaven and entered the presence of God to intercede for his people. The redemption he achieved was not temporary, as in the Temple ritual, but eternal. For this reason, when Jesus was crucified, the curtain in the temple was torn from top to bottom (Matt. 27:51), showing that it was God's work. The way into God's presence is now permanently open for those he loves. Jesus is our High Priest forever.

To my sorrow, I still think and do those things that displease him, but I come to my Heavenly Father with a sincere heart in full assurance of faith (Heb. 10:22). I confess my sins, and am justly forgiven. How? Because Jesus was my substitute, paying my debt in full. God does not punish twice for the same offence (1 John 1:9).

10.

I Love Jesus Because
He Adopted Me into His Family

TO BE BORN WITH A SILVER SPOON IN ONE'S MOUTH means to be born into a wealthy family. The idea is that the baby is rich as soon as he is born. The saying comes from the custom adopted by rich couples of giving a silver spoon to their baby at his christening. The poor could not afford it.

Comparatively speaking, few babies born into this world have a silver spoon in their mouths. Yet some who are born in adversity are destined for wealth and greatness. Baby Moses for example, had a very inauspicious start in life. Pharaoh, king of Egypt, in an attempt to reduce the strength of the Israelite slaves, issued a decree that all male babies be killed at birth. A Levite woman gave birth to a baby boy and was determined to defy the king's decree. But the time came when she could hide the child no longer, so she put him in a basket and placed it in the reeds of the river Nile.

The account of his discovery never fails to move me. Pharaoh's daughter went down to the Nile to bathe and saw the basket in the reeds. When she opened it and saw the child, she felt sorry for him. Moses' sister, who was evidently watching from a convenient distance, offered to get one of the Hebrew women to nurse the baby and the princess agreed. The obvious choice was the baby's mother! So, unknown to the princess, the mother was being paid to nurse her own son! (Exod. 2:1-10)

A slave child, sentenced to death by the king and being brought up in his palace is remarkable to say the least. Today, because of the infighting among the English Royal Family, it may not sound very attractive. In the case of Moses, however, it was a lifeline. He greatly benefited by it, and so did the Children of Israel. Moses was chosen by God to lead them out of oppression to the border of the Promised Land. God 'raises the poor from the dust and lifts the needy from the ash heap; he seats them with princes...' (Ps. 113:7).

God did something even more remarkable for me. His Son took pity on my desperate plight, rescued me from oppression and uncertainty, and adopted me into his family. He seated me with Christ in the heavenly realms in order that in the coming ages he might show the incomparable riches of his grace expressed in his kindness to me in Christ Jesus (Eph. 2:5-7).

He is still doing it. Every day, countless numbers of poverty stricken born again individuals are being adopted into the family of the King of kings. Once the 'objects of wrath', they are born of the Spirit into the family of God (John 1:12). They bring nothing in their hands, and yet no one was ever born richer. Once both dirty and naked, they are now washed clean and dressed in royal robes (Rev. 7:14). Once castaways under sentence of death, they now have a glorious inheritance in heaven. Once starved of pity, the King of kings now cares for them himself. Once unknown, they are born into a family so big that their brothers and sisters, all royals, cannot be counted (Rev. 7:9).

If you ask me how I know this, I shall not find it easy to answer. It is a bit like trying to explain colour to a blind man. The only way to appreciate the intensity of the colour red for example, and how it relates to other colours, is to have eyes to see it. Any attempt to describe the colour to a sightless person would merely expose the limitation of words. So it is with this question. But let me try anyway.

You may think that all the improvements in my life over the past six decades give me the right to call God Father. You would be wrong! No one can earn that right. All the changes in my life for good are God's work anyway. Just as I did not merit the privilege of calling my human father 'dad', so I cannot earn the privilege of calling God 'Father'.

Nor was it because of my dad's influence that I was able to call him 'father'. Other men also had a powerful influence on me but I never called them 'dad'. No, it was because it was natural for me because I was born into the family. I needed no persuasion. I could not call anyone else 'dad' because I did not have the same bond with any other man.

I have recollections of being in a crowd – I think I was about seven or eight years old – and I grabbed a man's hand and called him 'dad'. The words froze on my lips as soon as I discovered my mistake, and I dropped his hand like a wet fish. You may say there are many children who now call a man father only to find out in later life that he is not their natural father, but exceptions make bad rules. In any case, there are no anti climaxes in God's family.

Nor do I need confirmation that God is my Father. The 'Spirit of sonship' (Rom. 8:15-16) makes it 'natural' for me to address God in this way. In other words, the Holy Spirit and my human spirit agree that I am God's child. With this comes the assurance that I am an heir of the glory to come – an heir of God and a co-heir with Christ (Rom. 8:17).

This being the case, all God's children are now my brothers and sisters, for everyone who loves the father loves his child as well (1 John 5:1). The fact that all God's children on this earth are still sinners makes our fellowship less than perfect, but it is a foretaste of heaven nevertheless. Many of these dear people whose friendship has meant so much to me, have gone ahead. They were saints in both name and character and left me a fine example to follow.

11.

I Love Jesus Because
He Will Never Let Me Go

A HEART-RENDING SCENE FROM A FILM sticks in my mind. I cannot remember the name of it nor anything about it except this: A young German Jew, having been brutally separated by the Nazis from the girl he loved, met her by 'chance' in a very crowded railway wagon that was taking them both to an extermination camp. The memorable scene captured the momentary surprise and joy as they recognised each other and their effort to join hands in the crush. It was a moment of joy not to last. Soon, they endured the horror of a second parting and never saw each other again. Fiction perhaps, but I have no doubt that such tragic events were fairly common for the Jews in those terrible days.

The horror of being parted forever from Jesus, after being loved by him, would be infinitely greater. A more dreadful prospect cannot be imagined. Thank God, this too is fiction (Rom. 8:38). Many believers inflict unnecessary anxiety upon themselves by rejecting this glorious truth. They do not comprehend what the death of Christ achieved for them. They have been taught to believe that Jesus merely made their salvation possible and that the rest is up to them. One error leads to another. Having believed the lie that they initiated the process that led to their salvation, they work on the principle that they are entirely responsible for keeping it up. They are millionaires living like paupers.

I cannot help wondering how those who believe this heresy can love Jesus without reserve. If I thought that what Jesus did for me on the cross was incomplete, my thanksgiving would be subdued. How could I worship him with a full heart, if I believed that repentance and faith were my own work? How could my thanks be genuine if faithfulness to my Lord were entirely my own responsibility? Left to my own devices, I would have fallen by the wayside long ago.

No! Jesus saves completely and those whom he saves he keeps securely. The faith that saves and the Spirit who keeps are God's gifts to his people, purchased for them by the blood of Christ. My trust rests on his sure promise: 'My sheep listen to my voice; I know them, and they follow me. I give them eternal life, and *they shall never perish*; no-one can snatch them out of my hand' (John 10:27-28). God is not in the business of saving people and then leaving them to their own devices. Why would he sacrifice his only Son for my salvation and leave the work unfinished? Why would he pre-destine me to glory before the creation of the world and then leave me to fulfil his purpose? It is a recipe for despair. If God cannot or does not keep his promises, we can only conclude that he is either impotent or untrustworthy, or both.

Yes, I do love Jesus, but that is not the basis of my security. His love for me is what guarantees my destiny. 'Who shall separate us from the love of Christ?' Paul demands. (He is talking about Christ's love for us and not ours for him.) Shall trouble or hardship be able to sever the relationship? No! Shall persecution? No! Shall the lack of food and clothing? No! Shall the threat of death? No! Shall the trials and tragedies of the present and the future? No! Shall Satan himself? No! Then, just to make sure he has not for-gotten anything, Paul adds: Shall anything else in all creation? The answer is still 'No!' (Rom. 8:35-39).

These confident assertions do not mean that I shall be spared these hardships. They are, however, a warranty that nothing in the universe will break the bond of love between Jesus and me. God knows my weakness. He knows that left to myself, the bright lights of the world would dazzle me. He is fully aware that I would yield to the evil suggestions of my sinful nature and the seductive allure-ments of Satan.

I have known people who say they are able to remain faithful to the Lord in their own strength. Such a claim is due to shameful arrogance or pitiful ignorance. The apostle John tells us that it is much easier to love people we can see than it is to love God whom we cannot see (1 John 4:20). We know how our love for others can fail under pressure. What then would happen to our faithfulness if we were left to love God in our own strength?

The conclusion of the matter is this: My salvation does not depend on me, but upon God. It rests on his power and his infallible and unchanging decree. What he begins he always completes. He does not leave the outcome of his Son's sacrifice to the whims of Tom, Dick, or Harry, even if they are redeemed. The wisest saint does not always know what is good for him.

Moreover, we know that Jesus is interceding on behalf of his people (Heb. 7:25). In particular, he is asking that all those who are given to him by his Father, may be with him in heaven and see his glory – the glory the Father gave him before the creation of the world (John 17:24). Since his prayers are always answered (John 11:42), what better guarantee could we have?

Some misguided individuals object to this teaching because they see it as a licence to sin. They regard it as a violation of their much-vaunted free will. Their objections betray their ignorance. God has never violated my will. He *never* forced me to do anything! What he has done – and how I love him for it – is graciously to show me what is good for me and then give me the desire and the strength to choose it. So yes, in a way he does control my will, but he never curtails my liberty. He graciously and lovingly works in me so that I want to do what he wants me to do (Phil. 2:13). This is perfect freedom.

Only those who are strangers to God's steadfast love can make the preposterous suggestion that such teaching encourages believers to be lazy or to do wrong. They do not understand that God-given love for Jesus carries with it a strong desire to please him. Sin and laziness are anathema to God's chosen ones.

12.

I Love Jesus Because
He Gave Me Many Precious Promises

A FRIEND OF MINE BORROWED A LARGE SUM of money from his wealthy uncle to help buy a house. Every time he made a repayment, his uncle gave him a receipt to keep things in order. After some time, however, the elderly uncle informed his nephew that since he was the only beneficiary of the will, there was no point in making out receipts. Although his uncle was a trustworthy man, my friend was not happy with this arrangement but was too embarrassed to disagree.

After much of the loan had been repaid, the old uncle met and married a widow. Shortly after, he fell sick and died. The will was never found – it was supposed to be in a box under the bed – and the widow (for the second time) refused to accept that any money had been repaid except that shown on the early receipts. A legal battle ensued but my friend lost and suffered severe financial loss.

A promise is as trustworthy as the person who makes it, or so it is said. In this case, however, the uncle was regarded as a very trustworthy man and yet failed to keep his promise because things were taken out of his hands. There is a lesson here on how not to conduct business, even between friends and relatives. But there is a much more important lesson. For a promise to be guaranteed, the person who makes it must not only be trustworthy but in absolute control of the future as well.

God is such a Person. His promises – whether they are the promises of God the Father or God the Son, are guaranteed. For no matter how many promises God has made, they are all confirmed in Christ (2 Cor. 1:20-21). God never changes. He is the same yesterday, today, and forever (Heb. 13:8).

God made his promises in the context of an agreement with his people – what the Bible calls a covenant. It is not like the agreement made between my friend and his rich uncle. Rather, it is based on God's will. He cannot die and his will cannot be lost.

He made a covenant with the first man Adam. It failed because it depended on absolute obedience to God commands, and through Adam's disobedience, sin came into the world. Thankfully, the covenant God has made with me does not depend on obedience. For this reason it is called the Covenant of Grace. I love Jesus because by his death he ratified the covenant and secured its blessings. This is why he referred to his own blood as 'my blood of the covenant' (Matt. 26:28). Through his death, there is forgiveness for all my sins.

Of course, a covenant always includes responsibilities as well as promises. Marriage is a good example, except that with marriage the covenant depends on the agreement of both parties. By contrast, God's covenant was drawn up entirely by him, and he remains faithful to it. Nevertheless, he expects me to live a holy life. Those whose lives do not change are not members of the covenant no matter what they may claim.

The promises of the New Covenant are called 'better promises' (Heb. 8:6) because they contrast with the covenant God made with Moses. That covenant was based on obedience to God's commandments. It failed because the people could not keep them. It failed also because its sacrificial rituals could not take away sin. Nevertheless, the covenant was all part of God's plan. Indeed all the covenants of the Old Testament are in line with his eternal plan of redemption. This is obvious when we realise that the covenants mentioned in the Bible are not an end in themselves, but a relationship with God to prepare his chosen people for their ultimate glory.

The prophet Jeremiah sets out the promises of the New Covenant or Testament: "'This is the covenant I will make with the house of Israel after that time," declares the LORD. "I will put my law in their minds and write it on their hearts. I will be their God and they will be my people'" (Jer. 31:33-34). This wonderful promise is central to the everlasting Covenant of Grace and occurs many times throughout the Bible. It was God's promise to Abraham and his spiritual children back in Genesis. It is re-affirmed several times in the Old Testament and reaches its glorious fulfilment in the new heaven and the new earth (Gen. 17:7; Rev. 21:3). In that day, nothing will tarnish our fellowship with God.

Of course, I share this privilege with millions of others. For when we speak of Abraham's 'spiritual children', we are thinking of the countless number of people who have the same faith as he did (Rom. 4:11-12). God accepted Abraham as a righteous man because of his faith. As the Bible puts it, his faith was 'credited to him as righteousness' (Gen. 15:6). All who belong to Jesus are children of Abraham because they too are justified before God by faith in Jesus. We are all heirs according to the promise (Gal. 3:29).

The apostle goes on to explain that it was not through keeping God's law that Abraham and his offspring received the promise that he would be heir to the world, but through the righteousness that comes by faith (Rom. 4:13). This is why I have a confident expectation that I will be heir of the new and perfect world. Along with every true believer, I stand as one of Abraham's successors. But let it be clearly understood that I am eligible for this honoured position only because the Lord Jesus secured the promises and removed the guilt that would have disqualified me.

Over my life, the covenant promises have been very precious to me. For example, as I explain later in this book, they proved to be a powerful weapon in my fight against the love of money. For when our eyes are fixed on Jesus and what he has promised, we find it impossible to focus on the miserable riches of this world. A firm trust in the promises of God is the most efficient way of weakening our attachment to this world.

I remember the old story of the little boy whose hand was stuck in a jam jar. His fist was clenched, as if tightly holding on to something, but he could not be persuaded to let go. Finally, someone offered him half a crown. Immediately, his hand came out, and the penny he was clenching fell into the bottom of the jar. The promise of something of greater worth caused him to lose his grip on the item of lesser value. So it is with the promise of eternal riches.

As I wait for the final fulfilment of the covenant promises – the return of our Lord Jesus Christ in glory – having his love in my heart (Rom. 5:5) is a delightful foretaste. One day, perhaps sooner than we think, the promise of universal happiness made to Abraham's children so long ago, will be realised. We look forward in faith and confidence to that city with foundations, whose architect and builder is God (Heb. 11:10). That this should now be the destiny of a sinner like me is beyond my comprehension.

In addition, there can be no mistake as to whom I belong. Just as a seal is attached to goods as a means of protection and authentication, so the Holy Spirit marks me out as one who belongs to Christ. To put it another way, just as buyers pay part of the cost of the goods in advance in order to secure them, so the Spirit is a deposit guaranteeing that I shall belong to Jesus forever. The redeemed Church of Christ is his possession, and no power in the universe can do anything about it (Eph. 1:13-14). He is precious to everyone who believes, and everyone who believes is precious to him.

13.

I Love Jesus Because
He Gave Me Eyes to See

SOME YEARS AGO MY WIFE AND I SOLD OUR HOUSE to a man who lived in a flat with a glorious sea view. From his window, he could look across the bay and see the coastline receding into the distance. With the constant changing of the weather, his view was never the same. One day the sea would be calmly reflecting the blue of the sky. Another day it would be rough with the seagulls floating on the wind making their familiar cry. I ventured to ask our buyer why he wanted to move. He replied in a rather disgruntled tone and in his Yorkshire accent: 'Who wants to look at aw that watter?'

There was a time when I did not appreciate God's creation. The beauty of the earth meant little or nothing to me because I was blind to it. However, the day when Jesus revealed himself to me and enabled me to see something of his own glory with the eye of faith, was also the day he opened my eyes to see the glory of the world he made.

An old hymn puts it in a nutshell: 'Heaven above is softer blue; earth beneath is deeper green. Something lives in every hue, Christless eyes have never seen.' That is exactly how it was with me. Everything appeared in a new light. Now, after more than six decades, my appreciation of God's handiwork has not dimmed. On the contrary, it is keener than ever.

I too live by the sea and I often think of that poor man who complained about the view from his window. Every time I walk along the cliff, which I do in all sorts of weather, 'aw that watter' with its changing moods, thrills me to bits. So much so that my anticipation of living in the beautiful new earth, the home of righteousness (2 Peter 3:13), becomes stronger by the day.

Not only were my eyes opened to the glory of the heavens and the earth, I saw my own body in a different light. For the first time, I knew what the Psalmist meant when he said, 'I praise you because I am fearfully and wonderfully made' (Ps. 139:14). The organisation and complexity of the human body far surpasses anything made by man. There was a time when I thought nothing of it, and would probably have ended up abusing it as so many people do. Indeed, I had already begun to do so. Now I see it as God's masterpiece, and know that I have a duty to look after it, especially now that it is the temple of the Holy Spirit (1 Cor. 6:19-20).

I also 'see' how wonderful it is to be able to reason, memorise, love, hate and so forth. We usually think of the brain as the thinking, reasoning, and memorising organ of the body, but which part of our anatomy do we use to produce the wide range of human emotions? We say they come from the heart, but we know that this is not the case. We talk about people dying from a broken heart, but only because we do not know how else to describe the condition. Which organ of my body creates courage or fear? When my spirit is low, where is the problem located?

Although my entire body is affected by my emotions, there is more to it than that. A very important part of me is not physical at all – the part we call the soul or the spirit, depending on the view we take of our make-up. And yet, even though I may think of my soul and body separately, I am still one complete person.

The pleasure of work and play and the joy of relationships also became more significant. Above all, the privilege of serving the Lord in a fallen world I see as priceless, creating in me a deep sense of fulfilment. Indeed, when I look back over my life and remember my sins and my limitations, I stand amazed at what Christ has achieved through me. This always turns to thanksgiving, which is so liberating.

I must not give you the impression that I never forget to give thanks. This serious omission occurred most often when I was not well and my spirit was depressed, as I shall explain later. It is probably a weakness I share with many of God's people. Thankfully, such trying times have usually been short.

Do I not see ugliness in the world? Yes, of course I do, but most of it is the work of men. I remember a local beauty spot where I used to walk as a boy. It was a little dell covered with gorse bushes and bluebells, and inhabited by various kinds of wild life. In the spring, the grass provided good nesting for the skylark whose song could always be heard overhead. I watched in sorrow as year by year an enormous waste tip from the local collieries gradually filled the dell until it disappeared altogether under the smouldering slag. The smell was dreadful.

Yes, and I also see the wreckage caused by acts of God, like the recent tsunami, the Pakistan earthquake and the hurricanes in the Gulf of Mexico. These tragic events are warnings of judgment and symptoms of the curse brought about by human sin. They will have no place in the new world, because every vestige of sin and death will be banished forever. Weeds, thorns, pain, the cruel sea, war and impurity will all belong to the past. The Scriptures describe it as the dwelling of God with men (Rev. 21 and 22).

I do not suggest that people who do not know the Lord Jesus have no sense of appreciation of the good things of this life. My point is this, to know Jesus sharpens our senses in this regard to a degree that cannot be achieved in any other way.

14.

I Love Jesus Because
He Shares My Suffering

I HAVE TO CONFESS THAT THERE HAVE BEEN TIMES, especially during an illness, when I have felt desolate. To say I have always been aware of God's presence would not be true. This does not mean that the promise of Jesus is invalid (Matt. 28:20). I do not doubt that he was with me even when he seemed so far away. But at the time such confident statements did not pass my lips.

The Psalmist speaks of this gruelling experience: 'When I was in distress, I sought the Lord; at night I stretched out my untiring hands and my soul refused to be comforted. I remembered you, O God, and I groaned; I mused, and my spirit grew faint. You kept my eyes from closing; I was too troubled to speak' (Ps. 77:2-4).

I once suffered a strange illness. The three hospital doctors who examined me differed in their diagnosis. I had no difficulty in identifying with the psalmist's complaint. I was troubled during the day and could not sleep at night. Although still able to speak, only complaints passed my lips. I did not refuse comfort, but certainly began to think it would never come.

I also know what it means to suffer as a Christian. Those who think the Christian life is a bed of roses are obviously not true Christians. To live for Christ means to suffer for Christ. Paul warns young Timothy that 'everyone who wants to live a godly life in Christ Jesus will be persecuted' (2 Tim. 3:12). Suffering is the pathway to glory (Rom. 8:17). It was so for Jesus. It is so for me.

Suffering of this kind arises from the enmity between the children of God and the children of the devil. Very early in the Bible, we are told that God put enmity between Satan (represented by the serpent) and the woman (Eve), and between his offspring and hers (Gen. 3:15). The children of Satan are all those who reject the truth and follow evil. The seed of the woman is Jesus, and all who belong to him.

This enmity exists wherever there are believers and unbelievers. It exists in the church, as I quickly discovered after my conversion. We should not be surprised at this because those who hated Jesus most were in the religious establishment. The people Jesus identified as the children of the devil were none other than the religious Pharisees (John 8:44).

It should be no surprise then, when I tell you that as a servant of Christ I have been the subject of poison pen letters, vicious insinuations, malicious attacks on my character. At times, I have not felt safe when alone. If you ask me where I endured the most vicious persecution, I would not hesitate to say that it was not in the barrack rooms of the British Army, but in the ministry of the Church of England. Of course, this is nothing in comparison with the sufferings of the apostles, nor indeed with the sufferings of believers in other parts of the world at the present time.

My suffering however is not meaningless. God has a purpose in it. He is not punishing me for my sins, but weaning me from this world and preparing me for glory. The apostle Peter urges believers to rejoice that we participate in the sufferings of Christ, so that we may be overjoyed when his glory is revealed (1 Peter 1:6-7). Regrettably, I have not always been able to rejoice in it, but looking back, I do count it an honour.

So yes, I have suffered grief in all kinds of trials, as the apostle Peter puts it. I have no doubt that these have come so that my faith, of greater worth than gold, may be proved genuine and may result in praise, glory and honour when Jesus Christ is revealed (1 Peter 1:6-7). Taking a broad view of my life, as I am able to do at my age, I am satisfied that all my trials have strengthened my faith. I see them all as blessings from above. If, in reality, some were scourges from below, then I have no doubt that the Lord permitted them and used them for my benefit. 'It was good for me to be afflicted so that I might learn your decrees' (Ps. 119:71).

15.
I Love Jesus Because
He Set Me Free from
Nominal Christianity

MANY PEOPLE THINK THAT A MERE PROFESSION of Christianity is sufficient. They take comfort from the fact that they belong to the Church even though they may never darken its doors. Those who do attend are no better off unless they abandon the idea that going through familiar forms of worship improves their chances of going to heaven. 'The Lord says: "These people come near to me with their mouth and honour me with their lips, but their hearts are far from me"' (Isa. 29:13).

A colleague of mine was the vicar of two parishes. The two ancient churches were situated in villages about two miles apart. After a survey of one of the churches, the tower was considered unsafe and the building had to be closed. The vicar made immediate arrangements for a minibus to collect the few people who attended, take them to the other church, and back again. No one complained.

Some months later however, complaints from the village folk came thick and fast. The news had leaked out that the church was to be demolished! The villagers started a 'save our church' campaign and its chairman told the vicar that he had no right to knock their church down, and they were going to fight. The vicar explained the minibus arrangements but the man was unmoved. 'You don't understand,' he said, 'we are not interested in going to church, but the building must be preserved.'

Apart from the grace of God, I could have ended up like that man. I thought of myself as a Christian even though I was still a blasphemer. I too would have felt threatened by any proposal to knock my church down. After all, was I not born into a church family? Did I not go to that church three or four times every

Sunday in my childhood? Why should they knock it down? And yet, at the age of sixteen, I was thoroughly bored by the services and already straining on the leash. To me, termination of the tedious routine was a happy prospect.

Jesus set me free from this hypocrisy, but not by leaving me to go my own way. By opening my mind to understand the Scriptures (Luke 24:45), he became so real to me that almost immediately, I became deeply concerned about the state of the church I attended. The worship came alive. The reading of the word captured my attention. The hymns began to have meaning. As for the sermon, I was able to tell at once whether or not the preacher was a faithful man.

During my ministry, I have met many whose Christianity is merely nominal. Like me, they were brought up in church, but unlike me, their eyes had not been opened. For some reason hard to understand, they had kept up their Sunday routine. The majority were more concerned with ritual than reality and with tradition than truth. They would fight like tigers to retain forms of words that were hopelessly out of date. To defend and confirm the gospel (Phil. 1:7), however was foreign to them.

I remember one churchman who was angry with me for reading from the Revised Standard Version of the Bible instead of the Authorised. Another protested strongly because I used a modern English version of one of the psalms. When I pointed out to him that newcomers in the church would not understand the old fashioned language, he retorted: 'They must learn just like we had to.' But when I asked him to tell me what a particular verse in the old version meant, he could not!

Why God should open my eyes and not theirs I cannot understand, for apart from God's grace I am no better. Yet, I cannot but love Jesus for what he has done.

16.

I Love Jesus Because
He Set Me Free to Serve

JUST OUTSIDE THE CITY OF JERICHO, a blind man was sitting by the roadside, begging. He heard a crowd of people coming and asked what was going on. He was told that Jesus of Nazareth was passing by. Immediately he shouted, 'Jesus, son of David, have mercy on me.' When he was told to be quiet, he shouted even louder, 'Son of David, have mercy on me.' When Jesus reached the spot, he stopped, and asked the blind man what he wanted. 'Lord, I want to see,' he replied. 'Receive your sight,' Jesus said. Immediately, the man's sight was restored (Luke 18:35-42).

What happened next? Some would suggest that since the blind man had as much right to sight as anyone else, he would only need to say 'thank you' and then get on with his life. Others would expect a more enduring acknowledgement of his indebtedness to Jesus. The truth is, the man was so overwhelmed with thankfulness, that he followed Jesus, praising God. Clearly, this was no temporary reaction. His life was never the same again.

Loving Jesus is not possible unless we know we are loved by him. The desire to follow him and to glorify God is born only in a heart that is full of gratitude for what he has done. It would be easier to jump over the moon than to serve Jesus with an ungrateful heart. For all those people who, like me, have been set free from spiritual blindness, a lifetime of devotion to Jesus is a very inadequate 'thank you'.

Unless you are a wise man, you would feel sorry for me if I told you that for almost seventy years, I have been God's slave. You would probably say (or think) something like this: 'Poor soul, you don't know what you are missing.' You would be totally oblivious to the fact that you, not me, would be the object of pity.

During my time in the British Army in the Second World War, I met many men who concluded that I was naïve about the ways of the world. They would say something like this: 'You don't smoke, you don't drink, and you don't sleep with women. Why don't you let yourself go a bit?' Here were men, offering the parts of their bodies in slavery to impurity and to ever-increasing wickedness (Rom. 6:19) and advising me to do the same. They sowed to the wind, reaped the whirlwind (Hosea 8:7), and fooled themselves that they were free. What blindness!

I recall one night during the war when a colleague was in a dreadful state after drinking too much schnapps. I stayed with him until he sobered up, and during that time, he was heartily wishing he had not 'let himself go'!

Of course, slavery to sin does not always lead to marital infidelity and unpleasant hangovers. It is possible to live an outwardly respectable life and still be in bondage. The religious Pharisees who opposed Jesus were the slaves of sin, but it showed itself in hatred, wilful blindness, and pretentious humbug.

By contrast, to be the slave of Christ is perfect freedom. Jesus said, 'If you hold to my teaching, you are really my disciples. Then you will know the truth, and the truth will set you free' (John 8:31-32). And Paul: 'But now that you have been set free from sin and have become slaves to God, the benefit you reap leads to holiness, and the result is eternal life. For the wages of sin is death, but the gift of God is eternal life in Christ Jesus our Lord' (Rom. 6:22-23).

In the minds of some, the fact that God has planned my life may add to the impression that I am not free. Programmed like a robot, they would say, to do exactly as its designer intended. Nothing could be further from the truth. Like all men, I have the power to choose, within limits, and I use it every day. When I choose to do anything, I am fully aware that I could have chosen to do something else. Obviously, I would not be free if I were forced to do what was against my own will.

Like everyone else in this world, what I do is determined by how I think and what I desire. The difference is this: By a miracle of God's grace, how I think and what I desire are being graciously brought into line with how God thinks and what he desires. That is why I love Jesus. To be free to go my own way would be slavery of the worst kind.

'Do people pick grapes from thornbushes, or figs from thistles?' Jesus asked. 'A good tree cannot bear bad fruit, and a bad tree cannot bear good fruit' (Matt. 7:16,18). The nature of the fruit depends entirely on the nature of the tree. Therefore, now that God has given me a new nature with the desire to serve him, that is what I do. He does not force me to do anything. Rather, he gives me his Spirit so that I am able to take great delight in being his bondservant. 'Where the Spirit of the Lord is, there is freedom' (2 Cor. 3:17).

Before Jesus found me, I was not free to serve him. My former habit of blaspheming his Name will illustrate the point. Being with friends whose mouths were equally foul aggravated my sin. It would have been easier to stop if I had kept better company. But that is just the point. I had no desire to keep better company. This sin, therefore, had absolute power over me (Jer. 13:23). But when the Spirit of Christ transformed my life, the company of blasphemers became intolerable overnight! I was free from the sin of blasphemy forever.

But the freedom Jesus gives is not only negative. He gives freedom *from* something and *to* something – freedom *from* condemnation, *from* the power of sin, and *from* the power of Satan, and freedom *to* love God and *to* serve him.

17.

I Love Jesus Because He Has a Plan for My Life

NO ONE CAN EVER LOOK BACK over a long life and say he has no regrets. A confession of my faults, shortcomings, transgressions, mistakes and imperfections would fill many A4 sheets of paper, using small font and single spacing. That would only include those things that come readily to mind. If it were possible to live my life over again, I would do many things differently, providing of course, that I could retain the wisdom I acquired on the first run.

I could, of course, fill many sheets of paper with the 'good' things I have done, and compare one with the other in the hope that the good will cancel out the bad. It would, of course, be a waste of time because even the good things were not good enough for God. Nothing I ever did was done from the purest of motives.

Yet the amazing truth is this – God has a plan for my life and has been working it out in detail over the years. Long before I was born, the life I was destined to live was in the mind of God. He has even used my sins to further his purpose and to teach me some valuable lessons on the way. Paul puts it like this: 'For we are God's workmanship, created in Christ Jesus to do good works, which God prepared in advance for us to do' (Eph. 2:10).

As a servant of Jesus Christ, I look back over many fruitful years of service, and look forward to sharing the glory of God (Rom. 8:17). But as I have said so many times in this book, what I have done has contributed nothing to my salvation. The apostle's words just quoted prove beyond any doubt that my privileged position is not something I have deserved. It must surely be obvious that since God 'prepared in advance' (Eph. 2:10) all the good things I have done, I cannot take any credit for it. God, in Christ, has made me what I am. That is why I love Jesus.

From the vantage point of old age, I am able to discern in some measure how God has been at work in my life. The benefits of many trials were not obvious at the time. On not a few occasions, I was very perplexed because the ordeal seemed to serve no purpose whatever. Now I am able to see these experiences in the light of the divine plan. My deepest regret is that I did not always trust in the Lord during those times, as I should have done.

This was particularly so in the matter of my call to the ministry. Soon after my conversion I became aware of an inner conviction that in due time, the Lord wanted me in the ministry of the church. Believe it or not, twenty-four years passed before I was ordained! In spite of the fact that everything seemed to work against it, the conviction deepened.

Two years after my conversion, I was called up, and spent the next five years in the British Army. On my demobilisation, I returned to the Methodist church where I was brought up only to find that I was not welcome. The minister was not exactly enamoured with evangelicals. I persevered for a few years but I was going nowhere. In the meantime, any vestige of the idea that I might end up in the Methodist ministry was blown away.

A further six or seven years of uncertainty passed. None of the churches in the town where I lived could be regarded as evangelical, and a newly formed branch of the National Young Life Campaign came to the rescue. During this time, even though I could not see my way forward, the conviction persisted. I began to feel that if the Lord really wanted me in the ministry, he had a strange way of going about it.

In any case, I was still making excuses. I did not have the right qualifications, I was too nervous to be a public speaker, I could not afford to pay for my training, and my parents were not keen on the idea. When the way forward finally became clear, I had a wife and family, and a hefty mortgage. This gave rise to more excuses, which at the time, I regarded as good reasons. How could I leave my wife and family without income for two years? Did Paul not say that the man who does not make provision for his own family is worse than an unbeliever (1 Tim. 5:8)? To trust the Lord in this situation was one of the biggest challenges of my life.

To cut a long story short, after attending an evangelical Anglican church for a few years, I was accepted for the ministry of the Church of England without having the minimum qualifications required. After two years training, I was ordained. On that day, my wife was in good health, and my children, now three in number, lacked nothing. The mortgage too was paid.

Over the years, my wife has been with me in the work, which meant that my salary as a clergyman was our only income. Although we could never claim to be rich, I put it on record that we have never lacked anything needful. 'The LORD has done this, and it is marvellous in our eyes' (Ps. 118:23). How I wish I had trusted him more.

I like to compare God's workmanship to the finding, cutting and polishing of a diamond. When Jesus found me, I was rough and dirty. My character reflected nothing of God's light. All the useless material – those grievous sins and bad habits – had to be removed before the cutting and polishing process could begin. Like a skilful lapidary, God had the finished product in his mind. He knew exactly what he would make of such unpromising material. Gradually, he knocked off the sharp corners, and began to shape the stone according to his plan. Then, using the trials and tribulations of life as the lapidary's wheel, he began to polish each facet so that something of his glory began to reflect.

The beauty of the perfect stone will not be seen in this life. But what God has achieved so far, gives me every confidence that what he has begun, he will certainly complete (Phil. 1:6). Through the coming ages, with the rest of God's masterpieces, I will be on display to demonstrate the riches of God's grace and wisdom to the angels and whatever other order of intelligent beings there might be. Paul calls them 'rulers and authorities in the heavenly realms' (Eph. 2:7 and 3:10).

Unlike the diamond, however, I have not been unresponsive. Nothing I have said must be taken to mean that I have been able to sit back and let God get on with it. No, I have been busy working out my salvation with fear and trembling, knowing that God has also been busy working in me so that my will and my actions conform to his purpose (Phil. 2:12).

I know what it means to share in his sufferings. For his sake, I have been on the receiving end of gross insults, not least from fellow ministers and bishops. I have been threatened, falsely accused, and tried in the fire. And I would do it all again for the Lord I love. Of course, I cannot go back, but I can look forward with confidence to the day when God's plan for me will be accomplished. Then, and only then, will his workmanship be complete.

18.
I Love Jesus Because
He Taught Me to Pray

PRAYER HAS ALWAYS BEEN A STRUGGLE. The ability to pray for hours on end is something I have never possessed. Many times, in the small hours, I have been awakened by the cold, after falling asleep on my knees. This puts me in the same category as the disciples of Jesus who could not keep awake when their Master was overwhelmed with sorrow at the prospect of the cross. The spirit has indeed been willing, but the body weak (Matt. 26:36-45).

But I have always taken the Lord's rebuke to heart and I have worked on the principle that this weakness of my nature is the very reason why I should persevere. In our old age, my wife and I keep up our ministry of prayer for friends and family, for people we know about but have never met, for government and nation and much more besides.

Where did it begin? To answer this question I must go right back to my early childhood. It must have been my mother who taught me to say the Lord's Prayer. I think she also taught me the following words: 'Gentle Jesus, meek and mild, look upon a little child. Pity my simplicity; suffer me to come to Thee.' The reason I sound a little hesitant is that these prayers go back to those early years before I started to remember anything. But who else could it have been but my mum?

I do remember mastering the words of both prayers so well, that when I was left to say my prayers on my own, it probably took me less than a minute to kneel down, say the words, and jump into bed. It could hardly be regarded as prayer but at least I could say 'yes' if my mother asked me if I had said my prayers.

The far greater benefit came later. As is often the case with children, the meaning of the words they learn is not immediately apparent. Once the words were fixed in my mind, they were never forgotten. Like dormant seeds, they waited until the conditions were right before springing into life. After being indelibly engraved on my mind for many years, the Lord's Prayer in particular began to bear fruit in my heart. Many times, I have had cause to thank God that I was taught to say the Prayer from early childhood.

My cause to be grateful was brought into sharp focus when, during the later years of my ministry, I was asked to take the morning assembly in the local day schools. Whenever I invited the boys and girls to join me in saying the Lord's Prayer, sometimes well over five hundred of them, they were unable to do so. In some schools, not even the teachers were able to say it. Indeed, some seemed to resent being asked. Usually it was a monologue by me.

Clearly, Jesus thought it was very important to teach his disciples to use the prayer, containing as it does, all the basics of Christian prayer. He was teaching them to recognise his Father as their Father. This in itself would have been astonishing to them; they would never have thought of God in this way but for Jesus. He knew how important it was for them to honour the Father's name and to pray that his kingdom may come. He wanted them to realise that the necessities of life – bread to eat, forgiveness of our sins (on condition that we have forgiven others) and deliverance from strong temptation – are God's gifts.

For me, prayer is one of the greatest privileges of the Christian life. I confess I am not proud of my achievement in the school of prayer. I cannot count the times in my life when I simply did not know what to say. Crises arose in my own life, in the members of my family, or in the church and nation, that were so complex, I had no idea what to ask.

It is just at this point, however, that I have been able to rejoice because, in common with every true believer, the Holy Spirit prays for me and with me. He knows what I do not know. He takes up my faltering prayer, like a lawyer acting on behalf of his ignorant client. He puts into words what I may feel but cannot express except in sighs and groaning, and he censors out what is not in harmony with God's will. And God, who searches my heart, knows exactly the requests the Spirit is making on my behalf, and approves it. This must be the case, because the Spirit always intercedes for me according to God's will (Rom. 8:26-27).

Although I cannot understand what is going on, I feel sure that my prayers are answered. A negative answer proves that my request is not in harmony with God's will, at least not at this time. This guarantees that neither I, nor those for whom I pray, can be harmed by my misguided requests. An affirmative answer proves the opposite (1 John 5:14), although there may be differences between my request and the answer.

What a great consolation this is! God has made provision for my weakness and ignorance. Charles Hodge, in his commentary on Romans expresses the privilege in these words: 'Heathen philosophers gave this (our ignorance) as a reason why men ought not to pray! How miserable their condition when compared to ours! Instead of our ignorance putting a seal upon our lips, and leaving our hearts to break, the Spirit gives our desires a language heard and understood of God' (Epistle to the Romans, Banner of Truth Trust, 1972).

In spite of the hard work that prayer is, and in spite of all the times when the heavens have seemed like brass, I love Jesus for teaching me to pray.

19.

I Love Jesus Because
He Taught Me to Love Others

ALTHOUGH I AM UNDER NO ILLUSION about the depravity of the human heart, the depths of hatred into which people sink never ceases to amaze me. I have known people to take offence at a careless word or action, and then bear a grudge against the offender for the rest of their lives. Nor am I under any illusion about the shameful ill feeling that often exists between Christians.

Nevertheless, since I became a Christian, I have had the privilege of knowing many people whose genuine love for others has been an example to me. All of them had a prior love and devotion to the Lord Jesus. Being gracious and loving to me, it was easy to love them in return. The individuals I have found it hard to love have usually been professing Christians who showed me little or no affection and apparently did not want any from me.

Before my conversion, if I had unresponsive friends, I would ditch them and find new ones. When I became a Christian, however, I could no longer do this. I had to learn how to forgive and to love the unlovely, especially now that they were my brothers and sisters in Christ. This has not been easy. I have found it easier on occasions to love friendly but godless people.

Of course, Jesus is my supreme example. His love and patience with his disciples was unending. Even after they had all forsaken him and fled, he was more than ready to forgive. 'As the Father has loved me,' he said to them, 'so have I loved you' (John 15:9). When evil men hurled their insults at Jesus, 'he did not retaliate; when he suffered, he made no threats. Instead, he entrusted himself to him who judges justly' (1 Peter 2:23).

With the help of the Holy Spirit within me, I have been able to understand much more of the love of Christ than would otherwise have been possible. Even so, I still cannot fully comprehend it. His love passes knowledge (Eph. 3:18-19).

So, I am not being arrogant when I say that I have learned a little how to love others as Jesus did. I bear no malice towards anyone in the world; not even towards those who have wronged me. This does not mean, however, that my love for others is now what it should be. On the contrary, I still have a lot to learn. But it does mean that my love for others, being so contrary to my sinful nature, is proof of God's work in me, and all the glory must go to him. Left to my own devices, the people who hated me would have been left in no doubt that the feeling was mutual.

Over a period of four years, a man I will call Sid, kept up a vendetta against me. He was a church member, and seemed to think it was his duty to make my life miserable. In some ways, he succeeded. I tried hard to get alongside him and win his friendship but without success. One day, several years after I had retired, the phone rang. To my surprise, it was Sid. He wanted to come over and see me because he had been feeling badly about the way he had treated me.

We went for a walk, and Sid poured out his grief over his behaviour and asked for forgiveness. Long before he came to the point, the tears were streaming down my face as my heart warmed to him. We gave each other a bear hug, and that was the end of the matter. I have no doubt whatever that if the many others who opposed my ministry with so much venom came to ask forgiveness, my response would be the same. That is what Jesus has done for me, and that's why I love him.

To love is to forgive. Jesus stressed the importance of forgiveness in the life of a believer. After teaching his disciples the Lord's Prayer, he emphasised the petition for forgiveness in these words: 'For if you forgive men when they sin against you, your heavenly Father will also forgive you. But if you do not forgive men their sins, your Father will not forgive your sins' (Matt. 6:14-15).

Some take this to mean that if forgiven sinners do not forgive, they will not be forgiven, which is both a contradiction and a mistake. In the Lord's Prayer, our prior forgiveness of others is assumed: 'Forgive us our debts, *as we also have forgiven our debtors.*' We may regard the petition as a test of the genuineness of our faith because Jesus always softens the heart of the man who trusts in him, no matter how hard it is. Therefore, those who do not forgive are not forgiven and therefore are not true Christians. To say I love Jesus when I harbour grievances against others is hypocrisy in all its ugliness.

Love for the unlovely then, is the essential response of the human heart to the love of God. I love Jesus because he first loved me. And because I love Jesus, I love all those who belong to Jesus (John 15:12; Gal. 6:10), however grumpy they may be. My heart also goes out to all those who suffer, and who in any sense of the word can be called my neighbours. What wonders God performs!

I should point out that my love for others is not merely a feeling. Although loving others may generate joy and happiness, it is primarily a duty. Love and obedience towards God can never be separated. 'If anyone loves me,' Jesus said, 'he will obey my teaching' (John 14:23).

'And now, O Israel, what does the LORD your God ask of you but to fear the LORD your God, to walk in his ways, to love him, to serve the LORD your God with all your heart and with all your soul, and to observe the LORD's commands and decrees that I am giving you today for your own good?' (Deut. 10:12-13).

20.

I Love Jesus Because
He Taught Me to Think

INTELLECTUALLY, MY BROTHER was streets ahead of me. The fact that he was born with good brains, and I only with average, was not a problem in itself. The real cause of my undoing was my deep-rooted reluctance to use what intelligence God had given me. By contrast, my brother needed no coercion. To find his name on the school examination results, I did not need to look further down the list than the first three. To find my name quickly, it was always easier to start at the bottom!

Common sense would indicate that this should have spurred me on to do better. On the contrary, it made me rebel even more. I did find it discouraging, but I was too proud to admit it. Instead, I put on a brave face – perhaps even a defiant one – so that my mischievous spirit and love of play continued to hinder my progress. Eventually, it reached the point where I was not particularly interested in learning anything.

To illustrate the point, my mum and dad wanted me to learn to play the piano and engaged a music teacher. He certainly persevered with me, but neither he nor my parents could persuade me to practise between lessons. After six months, my dad decided it was a waste of money and my teacher was given the sack!

When I became a Christian, some of my attitudes were slow to change, but not this. The first sign of the revolution came before my conversion when I began to think seriously about my position. No doubt, this was the Holy Spirit at work. In the days following my conversion, I woke up to the fact that I had been a fool. Who else but God could have so suddenly made me eager to read and learn? Who else but he could have created that insatiable desire to restore the years the locust had eaten (Joel 2:25)? Now, after all these years, the yearning for learning is as strong as ever.

I am not talking about stuffing my head with useless information. Education is not merely gathering knowledge but learning how to use it. It is about acquiring the ability to think. It does not necessarily make men good. If they are devils to begin with, it will turn them into clever devils. Jesus is the one who makes men good. He is the one who taught me to think and to use my knowledge for the glory of God.

For many years, I have been impressed by the way Jesus taught his disciples to observe and think. 'Do not worry about your life, what you will eat or drink; or about your body, what you will wear. Is not life more important than food, and the body more important than clothes? Look at the birds of the air; they do not sow or reap or store away in barns, and yet your heavenly Father feeds them. Are you not much more valuable than they?' (Matt. 6:25-26). This command has always meant a lot to me. Through it, I learned to use my eyes and my reasoning powers in a practical way.

Finally, just as Jesus opened the minds of his disciples, so they could understand the Scriptures (Luke 24:45), so he has opened my mind for the same purpose. My capacity to understand God's word is one of God's most precious gifts. Where, I wonder, would I have been without that ability? 'The entrance of your words gives light,' says the Psalmist, 'it gives understanding to the simple' (Ps. 119:130, NKJV).

My appetite for God's word has grown enormously over the years. It is still my constant delight. I identify with Job when he said: 'I have treasured the words of his mouth more than my daily bread' (Job 23:12). Jesus changes brains as well as hearts!

21.
I Love Jesus Because
He Supports Me in Temptation

THE TENDENCY TO THINK that my temptations were greater than anyone else's, was one of my failings. When under pressure, I would try to convince myself that I would have a better excuse than others if I were to give in. When this happened, the words of Paul would come rushing to mind like a faithful sentinel: 'No temptation has seized you except what is *common to man*. And God is faithful; he will not let you be tempted beyond what you can bear' (1 Cor. 10:13).

The deceitfulness of my heart is such that I have a surprising ability to justify what I know to be wrong. Experience has taught me that strong temptation can affect the mind to the point where it no longer functions as it should. I am certainly not proud of this, but it has helped me to show compassion to my fellow believers when it is obvious that they are in the same situation.

Experience has also taught me that it would be the height of folly to think that I am no longer prone to give way to temptation, even in my old age. Having learned a lot about myself, I have less confidence than ever in my own ability to cope with it. My sinful nature plagues me constantly and my adversary the devil never gives up. He may change his tactics as I grow older, but he never stops trying to exploit the chinks in my armour. If left to fend for myself, he would soon find the weak spots.

I have learned that temptation can be fierce – very fierce. The fight against it can be long and hard. Of course, a lot depends on what sort of temptation it is. In some temptations, God provided a way of escape as he promised (1 Cor. 10:13), but to my shame, I did not always take advantage of it. In other circumstances, however, there has only been one option – to stand and fight.

I love Jesus because he is able to sympathise with me in my weakness. He has been tempted in every way, just as I am, but without giving way (Heb. 4:15). Because he always overcame it, he is the only one who fully understands it, and who has the ability to see me through it.

I love him too because his Spirit helps me in my weakness. I have no illusions. I know that when I want to do good evil is right there with me (Rom. 7:21), but the Spirit strengthens me in my fight against temptation, no matter from which quarter it comes – the allurements of the world, the sinful tendencies of my own nature, or the sinister devices of Satan himself.

The example Jesus has left for me to follow is also a cause of thanksgiving, not least because I know that if he was tempted by the devil, then that fiend will certainly not leave me alone. The way Jesus used the word of God when facing the temptations of Satan (Matt. 4:7,10) has also been a powerful influence in my life. I have lost count of the times I have done the same thing to fight off the enemy (Eph. 6:17).

Before my conversion to Christ, temptation defeated me on a regular basis. My upbringing provided some restraint but it did not create a desire to maintain the family standard. Indeed, I found the restraint irksome. Jesus has done for me what no other could do. He has given me a strong desire in my inner being to do what is pleasing to him. That desire, together with my knowledge of the wiles of the devil, ensures that when temptation comes, I know where to go.

22.
I Love Jesus Because He Delivered Me from the Love of Money

MY WIFE OFTEN ASKS ME to remove stains from clothes and furnishing materials. I try to determine what caused the blemish and then apply the appropriate stain remover. Some marks disappear at the first application, but others are more stubborn and need repeated treatment. Some are so difficult to remove, I have to resort to bleach, and even then, the result is hardly satisfactory.

Sinful habits are similar. The believer finds that some are quickly removed, but others take longer; sometimes much longer. Indeed, some moral weakness in his character may be so deep-rooted, that it may plague him for life. We are all different in this respect. I have had Christian friends who found it hard to stop smoking, others to stop swearing, yet others to control their temper. With me, the change in these areas was swift and permanent. If, however, you ask me to confess to one sin that has been hard to mortify, without hesitation I would say it was the love of money.

My parents often teased me about my childhood aspiration to own a Rolls Royce. They regarded it as a childish dream that would be forgotten when I grew older and had to face reality. My ownership of an old 1939 Rover, then regarded as the working man's Rolls, was the nearest I ever came to fulfilling the dream. I bought it for £300 and sold it thirteen years later for £14. Nevertheless, there was more to my hankering after wealth than a passing childish desire.

Most children are selfish by nature, and I was certainly no exception. In my teenage years, I became a little more skilled in covering it up, but I certainly did not conquer it. The love of money, even though I did not have much of it, was evidently deeply rooted in my sinful nature.

Until the Lord drew me to himself, I did not have a conscience
about it. But then it sprang to life. I began to feel badly about it.
Paul's words about God loving a cheerful giver (2 Cor. 9:7) never
failed to create a feeling of self-loathing, for the simple reason that
I was not cheerful about my giving. If Paul had learned how to be
content whatever his financial circumstances (Phil. 4:11), why was I
so slow to learn the lesson? I made valiant efforts to discipline myself in the matter, but it took me many years to accept the principle
of tithing my income, and even then, I never found it easy to do so
with a cheerful spirit.

It was for this reason that finance became a heavy but unnecessary burden when I faced up to my conviction that I should become a minister of the gospel. I felt suspended between my desire
to be successful in business on the one hand, and my clear calling to
abandon it on the other. The thought that I would never be rich if I
obeyed the calling depressed me.

Deliverance came through my wife. The Lord gave me a woman who had never been hooked on the love of money. During the
testing time before I gave up my job to go into training, she suffered
no misgivings in the matter. She has cheerfully accepted the hard
times when we had no money to speak of, and yet, all through it she
remained a cheerful giver.

As I come nearer to the end of my life, I am thankful that God
never allowed this vile sin (1 Tim. 6:10) to master me (Rom. 6:14).
The warnings of Scripture served their purpose. The rich young
ruler was deceived into thinking that his money was of more value
than treasure in heaven (Mark 10:17-22). The rich man in the par-
able who built bigger and bigger barns to store his wealth was not
rich toward God (Luke 12:16-21). Thankfully, I was delivered from
such folly.

More than anything else, my interest in worldly wealth has
faded because my appreciation and expectation of the eternal inheritance Jesus has given me have gone so deep into my soul. These
heavenly riches fall into two categories – those I now possess and
those he has promised. Of the first kind, I am rich in grace. That is
to say, God has removed my sins as far away as the east is from the
west; he has poured out his love upon me, and has granted me the
precious gift of his Holy Spirit to guide and strengthen me. He has

adopted me into his family so that I have so many Christian brothers and sisters they cannot be counted. In addition, the privilege of serving the church is something I would not have missed for all the gold in the Bank of England.

Of the second kind, a book could be written. Jesus has gone to prepare a place for me so that I have a permanent home in heaven. I have the firm promise of a resurrection body like the glorious body of my risen Lord Jesus, free from pain and decay (see the last chapter). And the expectation of a new earth, the home of righteousness, in which to live in perfect peace (2 Peter 3:13). Best of all, I shall see Jesus as he really is and be changed into his likeness. This is the zenith of my hope. No stronger antidote to selfishness exists.

With this bright future, do you wonder that my attachment to worldly possessions is being severed? It has been a constant struggle, but the riches Jesus secured for me have always been in my view. With such unfailing grace and endless mercy, how can I but love him? No sin is too stubborn for God's grace.

23.

I Love Jesus Because
He Will Give Me a Body Like His

I HAVE A COLLEAGUE WHO USED TO THINK NOTHING of staying up all night to meet a deadline. In his college days, he would swot all night and then sit exams the next day. By contrast, I am one of those who needs at least eight hours sleep. On the few occasions I have tried to work late, my forehead was in danger of making contact with the cold steel of the typewriter.

Whenever I was called out in the middle of the night, which, thankfully, did not happen frequently, I was like a zombie the next day. When I was unable to take my day off, which did happen frequently, I soon began to feel drained.

According to my doctor, it was the stress of the job that caused a heart attack which put me out of action altogether for several months. It shortened my stickability span permanently. I have almost forgotten what it was like not to have angina. The limitations of the body have certainly curtailed my contribution to the cause.

Things have not improved. If I sit at my computer for more than three hours these days, I am exhausted. This is probably because I have only one main artery in my heart functioning normally, and the medics say I am too old to take the risk of an operation. This condition, together with the complication of diabetes, necessitates a daily intake of pills which, when laid out on the breakfast table, look like an assortment of dolly mixtures!

Some plumbing had to be done in my waterworks to keep it functioning. I certainly do not get value for money when I pay the full price for my regular dental check up. There are more spaces than teeth, and it doesn't take my dentist more than a minute. My hair too grows only at the back and sides. My wrinkles are like furrows and in places my skin begins to look and feel like crêpe paper.

Thankfully, the grey matter still functions reasonably well, except that I need more megabytes for my short-term memory. Like everyone else in this world, I am slowly wasting away (2 Cor. 4:16).

How depressing you say? No, not really. The terrible thought of being in this position with no hope for the future would be very depressing. Indeed, I often wonder how unbelievers cope with old age. Perhaps they try not to think about it. Perhaps they fill their minds with other matters of the moment.

Thank God, it is not so with me. I am fully persuaded that when I leave this mortal body I shall be at home with the Lord (2 Cor. 5:8). On that great day when Jesus comes again, my body, along with the bodies of his redeemed people from every tribe and nation, will be raised imperishable. It will be refashioned like his glorious body (Phil. 3:21).

Then, I shall have the ability to glorify God, as I ought. I shall enjoy the perfect fellowship of all who are redeemed, and I shall take pleasure as never before, the glory of a new world. Tiredness, pain, tears, mourning and death itself will be banished forever (Rev. 21:4). The thrill I feel at this prospect of complete fulfilment and perfect happiness in the presence of Jesus, my Lord and Saviour, is indescribable.

'But' you say, 'how can God do this? What about Christians whose bodies have been cremated and their ashes scattered to the four winds? What about those who were blown to bits during war?' No answer to these questions will ever satisfy you if you are an unbeliever. But those who trust in Almighty God have no problem. We know that the Lord Jesus Christ who created all things and holds them together (Col. 1:16-17), has the power to bring everything under his control (Phil. 3:21).

Lord! It is my chief complaint
That my love is weak and faint;
But I love you and adore:
O for grace to love you more.

WILLIAM COWPER
(1731-1800)